W9-BDK-996

Cool Board Tricks

Ellen Labrecque

Raintree

Chicago, Illinois

© 2013 Raintree
an imprint of Capstone Global Library, LLC
Chicago, Illinois

To contact Capstone Global Library please phone 800-747-4992, or visit our website www.capstonepub.com

All rights reserved. No part of this publication may be reproduced or transmitted in any form or by any means, electronic or mechanical, including photocopying, recording, taping, or any information storage and retrieval system, without permission in writing from the publisher.

Edited by Rebecca Rissman, Daniel Nunn, and Adrian Vigliano
Designed by Cynthia Della-Rovere
Picture research by Elizabeth Alexander
Production by Alison Parsons
Originated by Capstone Global Library Ltd.
Printed and bound in China by China Translation and Printing Services Ltd.

16 15 14 13 12

10 9 8 7 6 5 4 3 2 1

Library of Congress Cataloging-in-Publication Data

Labrecque, Ellen.

Cool board tricks / Ellen Labrecque.

p. cm.—(Try this at home!)

Includes bibliographical references and index.

ISBN 978-1-4109-5002-4 (hb)—ISBN 978-1-4109-5009-3 (pb)

1. Skateboarding—Juvenile literature. I. Title.

GV859.8.L33 2013

796.22—dc23   2012014382

Acknowledgments

The author and publisher are grateful to the following for permission to reproduce copyright material: © Capstone Publishers pp. 9 b, 8, 9 t, 10 t, 10 b, 11 t, 11 b, 12 t, 12 b, 13 t, 13 b, 14, 15 t, 15 b, 16, 17 t, 17 b, 18 t, 18 b, 19, 22, 23 t, 23 b, 24 t, 24 b, 25, 26 t, 26 b, 27 t, 27 b (Karon Dubke); Getty Images pp. 7 (LatinContent), 20 (Adie Bush/Cultura); Shutterstock pp. 4 (© Galina Barskaya), 5 (© Vladimir Ivanovich Danilov), 6 (© goldenangel), 28 (© Ipatov), 29 (© TEA); SuperStock p. 21 (© UpperCut Images). Design features reproduced with the permission of Shutterstock (© charles taylor), (© Benjamin Ordaz), (© optimarc), (© optimarc), (© Merve Poray), (© Nicemonkey), (© Merve Poray).

Cover photograph of a skateboarder in mid-air reproduced with permission of Corbis (© Erik Isakson/ Blend Images).

Every effort has been made to contact copyright holders of any material reproduced in this book. Any omissions will be rectified in subsequent printings if notice is given to the publisher.

All the Internet addresses (URLs) given in this book were valid at the time of going to press. However, due to the dynamic nature of the Internet, some addresses may have changed, or sites may have changed or ceased to exist since publication. While the author and publisher regret any inconvenience this may cause readers, no responsibility for any such changes can be accepted by either the author or the publisher.

Bloomington, Chicago, Mankato, Oxford

Contents

Some words are shown in bold, **like this**. You can find out what they mean by looking in the Glossary.

Let's Cruise!

It's one thing to roll along on a skateboard. It's a whole different story to fly high and pull off a sick move! Want to wow your friends while riding? This book can show you how.

4

With a bit of practice, soon you will be performing moves you have only seen in magazines or at your local skate park. Let's cruise!

Be Safe!

Mastering a new skateboarding trick requires a lot of practice and patience. After all, performing skateboarding tricks can be an easy way to hurt yourself. Before you start, you must have the right safety gear.

Only skate in places that are safe, free of cars, and legal for skateboarding. You should always wear a helmet and knee and elbow pads when riding. Make sure you buy a helmet designed just for skateboarding and pads that fit snugly.

The Ollie

Level of difficulty:
Easy

The ollie is a no-handed **aerial**. Place your front foot mid-board and your back foot on the back. Press down with your back foot to lift the front of the board.

 STEP **1**

Jump up in the air. Drag your front foot toward the front as you lift.

STEP 3

Bring the board to a level position. Pull your knees to your chest in mid-air. Keep your arms out for balance.

9

Boardslide

Level of difficulty:
Medium

Approach a rail for your boardslide. Do an ollie, and turn the board at a sharp angle in either direction.

STEP 1

STEP 2

Plant your feet firmly and slide your board along the rail's edge.

10

As you approach the end of your slide, shift your weight back and turn your board back to a riding direction.

Land with both feet at the same time and your knees bent.

Insider tip:

Another great place to try a boardslide is a curb.

Drop In

STEP 1

The drop in is how skateboarders enter **half-pipes**. Dropping in can be scary at first. Put your **tail** on the edge of the half-pipe, with both sets of wheels almost into the ramp.

STEP 2

Put one foot on the back of the board and the other in front.

12

STEP 3

Shift your weight to the front of the board.

STEP 4

Your shoulders stay **parallel** with the board as you ride down.

Insider tip:

Don't stand at the top of the ramp and think. Just go for it as soon as you're there.

13

Manual

Level of difficulty:
Easy

STEP 1

Balancing on your back wheels while rolling is called a manual. While rolling, your back foot should be on the **tail** of your board, and your front foot should be in the middle. Shift all your weight to the back foot, while your shoulders lean forward.

STEP 2

Your board will rise up in the front, and you will cruise on the back wheels.

STEP 3

When you are done, shift your weight back to your front foot and ride away.

Insider tip:

The manual is about balance. Stick your hands out to your sides to help you stay up.

Frontside Air

Level of difficulty:
Hard

You'll feel like you are flying when you do a frontside air! This trick is done on a **half-pipe**. Drop in and ride up the other side of the ramp.

STEP 1

Your feet stay on the board for the entire trick. As your back wheels lift off the ramp's edge at the top, grab the front of the board with your trailing hand as you fly into the air.

Bend your knees to your chest and turn your body back down the ramp.

Use your lead hand to guide you, and keep your knees bent.

Keep your weight in the center of the board and extend your legs to nail the landing.

Cruise on down the ramp and ride away smoothly.

Let's Snowboard!

Snowboarding is a great way to stay fit during the cold months. But the sport can be dangerous. Wearing a helmet is a must. You can also buy snowboarding pants with pads built into them.

Wear wrist guards to prevent broken wrists and forearms on falls. And, don't forget to strap on goggles. They'll keep the snow out of your eyes and protect you from tree branches on your way down the slope.

Nail a Jump

STEP 1

Level of difficulty:
Medium

Practice your jump standing still on flat ground. Bend your knees and quickly spring up. Both ends of the board should rise to the same height.

STEP 2

Next, try "popping" while you are riding. Get nice and low and pop into the air with both feet.

STEP 3

Try a jump on an actual ramp. Choose a small jump and **crouch** low as you approach the takeoff.

STEP 4

Keep your shoulders **parallel** to the board. Pop up as your front foot reaches the top of the jump to fly into the air.

STEP 5

Bring your knees up to your chest to get more height.

Land on your whole board, not the back or front first.

Insider tip:

Your hands should stay at the front and back of your board. This will keep you balanced.

Indy Grab

Level of difficulty:
Medium

STEP 1

Ride toward the jump
at medium speed.
Bend your knees to
get ready. When you
reach the top, take off
into the air.

STEP 2

While in the air,
kick your feet
back like you're
on your knees.

Grab with your rear hand on the front side of the board.

Hold the grab as long as you can, then let go. Release in time to land. Bend your knees to absorb the shock.

27

Lookin' Cool!

Doing skateboarding and snowboarding tricks isn't just about the tricks. It's also about looking good! Here are some tips to look your best.

1. Get the basics down.

2. Wear bright colors on the slopes.

3. Add your own style to tricks. You can make tricks all your own.

4. Put safety first. Nobody looks good crashing.

5. The more fun you have, the better you'll look.

Glossary

aerial trick done in the air

crouch stoop or bend low

half-pipe U-shaped ramp used by skateboarders and snowboarders for tricks

parallel extending out in the same direction

tail rear part of a skateboard or snowboard

Find Out More

Books

Gifford, Clive. *Skateboarding*. New York: DK Publishing, 2006.

Murdico, Suzanne. *Snowboarding: Techniques and Tricks*. New York: Rosen Publishing Group, 2003.

Sohn, Emily. *Skateboarding: How It Works*. Mankato, Minn.: Capstone Press, 2010.

Internet Sites

Facthound offers a safe, fun way to find Internet sites related to this book. All of the sites on Facthound have been researched by our staff.

Here's all you do:

Visit www.facthound.com

Type in this code: 9781410950024

Index